THE SECOND BOOK OF MEZZO-SOPRANO/ALTO SOLOS

PART II

compiled by Joan Frey Boytim

G. SCHIRMER, Inc.

DISTRIBUTED BY

HAL•LEONARD®
CORPORATION
7777 W. BLUEMOUND RD. P.O. BOX 13819 MILWAUKEE, WI 53213

PREFACE

Many teachers have expressed the desire to have a second volume to complement *The Second Book of Solos* series for those high school and college students studying more advanced student literature. In my studio, I have found that students using the four volumes of *Easy Songs for Beginning Singers* in seventh and eighth grades move very easily into *The First Book of Solos* and *The First Book of Solos–Part II* in ninth and tenth grades. Several of my students have moved into *The Second Book of Solos* as early as eleventh grade. They would find the variety of *The Second Book of Solos–Part II* a welcome addition to their repertoire for eleventh and twelfth grades. With many of today's college freshmen using *The First Book of Solos* and *The First Book of Solos–Part II*, *The Second Book of Solos* and this new *Part II* will prove to be a great launching pad of further new repertoire for freshman and sophomores.

The songs introduced in this volume are on comparable levels of sophistication and musical difficulty with those found in *The Second Book of Solos*, and could be used at the same time to provide more variety of repertoire. Each voice volume has representative English, American, Russian, Italian, German, French, sacred, oratorio, and Gilbert and Sullivan selections not used previously in any of my other anthologies. There are a number of out-of-print songs which deserved to be reissued, and quite a number of unfamiliar songs which should find a place in student repertoire.

In these volumes we have been able to include pieces from more contemporary composers such as Barber, Bax, Bowles, Chanler, Duke, Dougherty, Hoiby, Ives, Griffes, Gurney, Lekberg, Sacco, Thomson, and Warlock. The relatively unknown French composer, Félix Fourdrain, is represented in three of the four volumes. These songs, as well as other unfamiliar French mélodies, have only been available in single sheet form and have never before had English singing translations. For these songs, a life-long vocal accompanist and retired French professor, Harry Goldby, has made very singable texts which relate very closely to the original poems. My excitement mounts when I think of those students who will enjoy learning many of these more unfamiliar songs, as well as those songs that have been difficult to find.

This set of four books will conclude the more advanced portion of this 16 volume basic series of teaching material for soprano, mezzo-soprano/alto, tenor, and baritone/bass (the four volumes of *The First Book of Solos*, the four volumes of *The First Book of Solos–Part II*, the four volumes of *The Second Book of Solos*, and now the four volumes of *The Second Book of Solos–Part II*). There are 528 different songs included in the 16 volumes, with an average of 132 songs of all varieties carefully chosen for content and suitability for each voice part. I only wish I had had all of these books for teaching when my studio began over 45 years ago!

Joan Frey Boytim
May, 2004

CONTENTS

AFFANNI DEL PENSIER
(O Agonies of Thought)

English version by Dr. Theodore Baker

George Frideric Handel
(1685-1759)

da - te-mi pa - ce almen,   da - te-mi pa - ce almen,   e
leave me in peace_ a-gain,   leave me in peace_ a-gain,   then

poi tor - na - te.   Af - fan -
turn and rend me.   O ag -

- ni del___ pen - sier,   un sol mo - men - to
- o - nies___ of_thought,   one mo-ment on - ly

da - te-mi pa - ce almen,   e poi tor - na - te,
leave me in peace a-gain,   then turn and rend___ me,

6

un sol mo - men - to da - te - mi pa - ce al -
one mo - ment on - ly leave me in peace a -

men, ___ e poi tor - na - te, tor - na - - -
gain, ___ then turn and rend me, one mo - - -

te, ___ e poi tor - na - te; Af - fan - ni del ___ pen - sier,
ment, then turn and rend me; O ag - o - nies ___ of thought,

da - te - mi pa - ce almen, e poi tor - na - te, e poi, ___
leave me in peace a - gain one moment on - ly, and then, ___

e po - i tor - na - te.
then turn_____ and rend_____ me.

AH, LOVE BUT A DAY!

Robert Browning

Amy Beach
(1867-1944)

Look in my eyes! Wilt

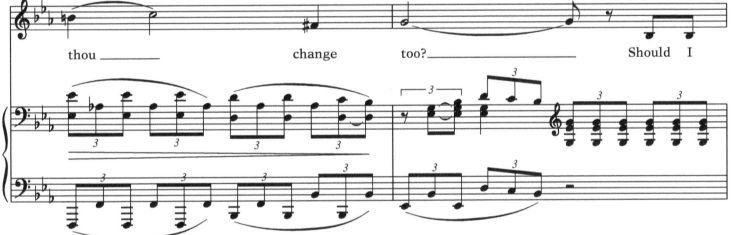

thou change too? Should I

fear sur-prise? Shall I find aught new In the

old and dear, In the good and true

ALL MEIN GEDANKEN
(All The Fond Thoughts)

Felix Dahn
English version by John Bernhoff

Richard Strauss
(1864-1949)

14

ALLERSEELEN
(All Soul's Day)

Hermann von Gilm
English version by Florence Easton

Richard Strauss
(1864-1949)

Tranquillo

Stell' auf den
Place here by

Tisch die duf-ten-den Re - se - den, die letz-ten ro - ten A-stern trag' her-
me the mi-gnon-ette so fra - grant, And close be-side them as-ters bright and

bei, und lass uns wie-der von der Lie - be re - den, wie
gay, And let us speak a-gain of love's sweet rap - ture, As

18

AS THOU WILT, FATHER

from *Gethsemane*

C. Lee Williams
(1853-1935)

20

AU JARDIN DE MON PÈRE
(In My Dear Father's Garden)

English version by Harry Goldby

Pauline Viardot
(1821-1910)

23

Trois jeu - nes de - moi - sel - les L'y si vont om - brai -
Three young and pret - ty maid - ens like to rest in its

ger; _____ Ay - mez - moy ma mi -
shade; _____ Love me please, dear - est

no ritard.

gnon - ne, Ay - mez - moy, sans dan - ger, _____ Ma mi -
sweet - heart, love me please have no fear. _____ You can

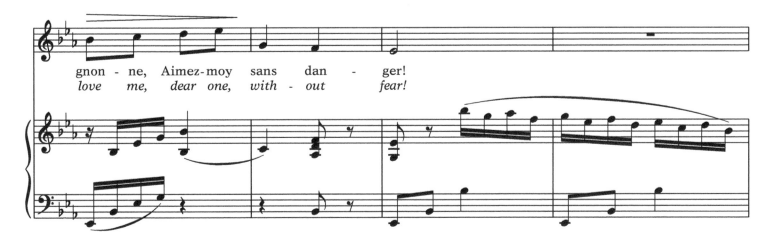

gnon - ne, Aimez-moy sans dan - ger!
love me, dear one, with - out fear!

Mi - gnon - ne, Ay - mez -
My dar - ling, love me,

moy! _____
please! _____

Trois jeu - nes de - moi - sel - les L'y si vont om - brai -
Three young and pret - ty maid - ens like to rest in its

ger; _____
shade; _____

Trois jeu - nes gen - tils -
Three young and hand - some

le Et la pri - ay de m'ai - mer! _____
and en - treat - ed her to love me! _____

Mon père est dans sa cham - bre,
My fa - ther's in his cham - ber

Al - lez lui de - man - der! _____
Go there and ask him now! _____

Ay - mez - moy, ma mi - gnon - ne, Ay - mez -
Love me please, pret - ty maid - en, come with

moi sans dan - ger. _____ Mon père est dans sa cham - bre, Al -
me have no fear. _____ My fa - ther's in his cham - ber, go

lez luy de - man - der... Et s'il en est con - tent, et
there and ask him now. And if he is con - tent, and

s'il en est con - tent, Et s'il en est con - tent, Je me veux ac - cor -
if he is well pleased, and if he is con - tent, then I too shall a -

der! _____
gree! _____

AVRIL
(April)

Rémy Belleau

Léo Delibes
(1836-1891)

Andantino quasi Allegretto

A - vril, _____ La
Sweet month! _____ which

grâce et le ris De Cy - pris, _____ Le flair et la douce ha -
to us dost bring The glad Spring, _____ Thy breath on Na - ture be -

lei - ne: A - vril, _____ Le par - fum des dieux, Qui des
stow - ing, Sweet month! _____ thy scents from a - bove, Which gods

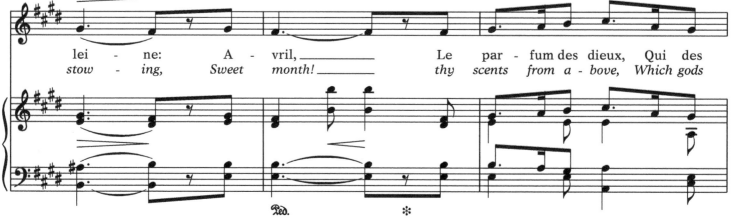

cieux,   Sen - tent l'o - deur de la plai - ne,   sen - tent l'o -
love,   Come o'er the plain to us blow - ing,   Come o'er the

deur de la plai - ne.
plain to us blow - ing.

A -
Sweet

vril, c'est ta dou - ce main, Qui du sein De la na - tu -
month! 'tis 'neath thy soft hand, Doth ex - pand Each op-'ning blos -

re,   des - ser - re U - ne___ moi - sson de sen - teurs   Et   de
som   and flow'r,   And   waft___ ed   up - on   the   air   Per - fumes

fleurs, __ Em - bau - mant l'air et___ la ter - re.   A -
rare, __ Their fra - grance do o - ver us show - er,   Sweet

vril_____   La grâce et le ris De Cy - pris. _____ Le
month! _____   Which   to   us dost bring,   The glad   Spring, _____   Thy

flair   et la douce ha - lei - ne.   A - vril; _____   Le par - fum des dieux, Qui des
breath   on Na - ture be - stow - ing,   Sweet month! _____   thy scents from a - bove Which gods

pas - sa - gè - res, Ces hi - ron - del - les qui vont, Et qui sont Du
win - ter fear - ing, See! how they come from a - far; And they are The

prin-temps les mes - sa - gè - res, Du prin-temps les mes - sa -
her - alds of spring - time near - ing, The her - alds of spring - time

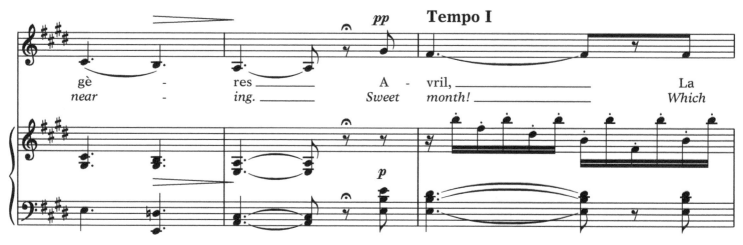

Tempo I

gè - res A - vril, La
near - ing. Sweet month! Which

grâce et le ris De Cy - pris, Le
to us dost bring The glad spring, Thy

THE AWAKENING

Edward Teschemacher

Eric Coates
(1886-1957)

When first you gazed on me, I on-ly knew _____ Your eyes were kind and lit with life's fair light, _____

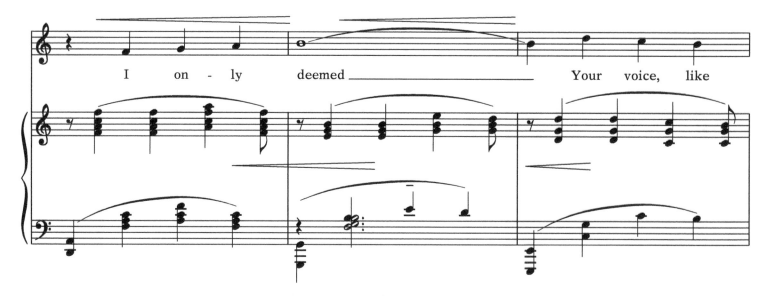

I on - ly deemed _____ Your voice, like

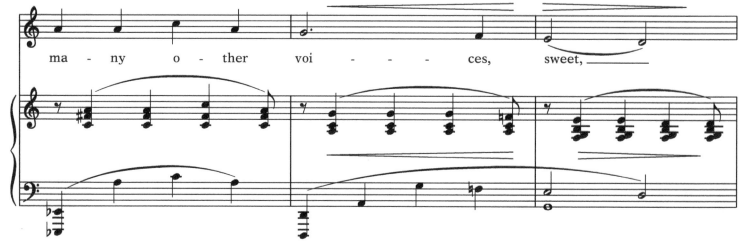

ma - ny o - ther voi - - ces, sweet, _____

And yet as I went sing - ing on my way, _____

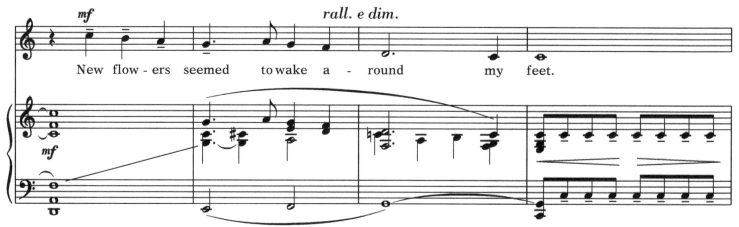

New flow - ers seemed to wake a - round my feet.

Poco più mosso

But when you came one day and saw my tears,

And your great ten - der - ness and hope made known,

Ah! then I knew that God, from all the

world, Had cho - sen you for me, _____ had

BEFORE MY WINDOW

Sergei Rachmaninoff
(1873-1943)

English version by Henry G. Chapman

40

CHANSON TRISTE
(A Song of Sorrow)

Jean Lahor
English version by M. Louise Baum

Henri Duparc
(1844-1933)

Lento affettuoso
sempre legatiss.

pp

dolciss.

Dans ton cœur dort un clair de lu - ne, Un doux
Moon - light full - ness thy heart il - lum - ing, Such as

clair de lu - ne d'é - té,_____
floods the fair sum - mer night,_____

poco cresc.

cresc.

Et pour fuir_____ la vie im - por-tu - ne
Ah! to flee_____ life's vain im - portun - ing,

poco cresc.

cresc.

Je me noie - rai _____ dans ta clar - té. _____
Would I could drown me in that pure light! _____

J'ou - blie-rai les douleurs pas - sé - es, Mon amour,
My despair - could I long - er fear it, O my love,

quand tu ber - ce-ras Mon tris - te cœur et mes pen - sé - es
when are cra - dled free from harms My wear - y heart and spir - it

44

45

pleins de tris-tes - ses, Dans tes yeux a - lors je boi -
sweet in their sad - ness, From thy lov - ing eyes my tired

rai Tant de bai-sers et de tendres - ses,
soul Draughts so di - vine shall drink of glad - ness,

Que peut-ê - tre je gué - ri - rai....
I perchance a-gain shall be whole.

CHERRY VALLEY

Joseph Campbell

Roger Quilter
(1877-1953)

heav-y boughs are crim - son - éd, crim -

- son - éd.

Now__ the low moon is look-ing through_____ The glim - mer of the

hon - ey dew. A

pet - al trem-bles to the grass,_____ The feet of fai - ries

pass_____ and pass._____

In Cher-ry Val - ley the cher-ries blow; The val-ley paths are white as snow;

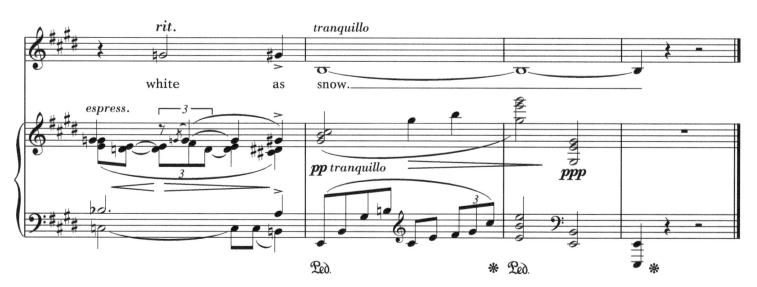

white as snow._____

DU MEINES HERZENS KRÖNELEIN
(Pride of My Heart)

Felix Dahn
English version by John Bernhoff

Richard Strauss
(1864-1949)

Du meines Her - zens Krö - ne-lein, du bist von laut' - rem
Pride of my heart, its crown, its joy, thou art a gold - en

Gol - de, wenn an - de - re da - ne - ben sein, dann
trea - sure, com-pared to thee, all is al - loy: none

bist du erst viel hol - de. Die an - dern tun so gern ge -
can thy vir - tues mea - sure. While o - thers boast with words of

DU RING AN MEINEM FINGER

Adelbert von Chamisso
English version by Frederic Field Bullard

Robert Schumann
(1810-1856)

Du Ring an mei - nem Fin - ger, mein gol - de-nes Rin - ge - lein, ich drü - cke dich fromm an die Lip - pen, dich fromm an die Lip-pen, an das Her - ze mein. Ich

Dear ring up - on my fin - ger, My dear lit - tle ring of gold, I press thee de - vot - ed-ly to my lips, De - vot - ed-ly now up - on my heart I hold. The

55

mei - nem Blick er - schlo - ßen des__ Le - bens un - end - li - chen,

taught me all the won - der Of__ Life and of Im - mor -

poco a poco più animato

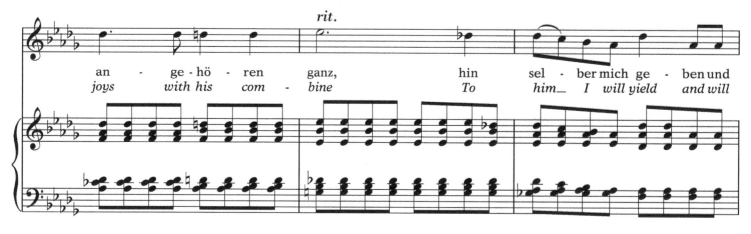

tie - fen Wert. Ich will ihm die - nen, ihm le - ben, ihm

tal - i - ty. I'll serve him glad - ly, I'll live for him My

rit.

an - ge - hö - ren ganz, hin sel - ber mich ge - ben und

joys with his com - bine To him__ I will yield and will

rit.

fin - den ver - klärt mich, und fin - den ver - klärt mich in sei - nem Glanz. Du__

find me il - lu - mined, and find me il - lu - mined in his__ fond glance, Dear__

a tempo

Ring an mei - nem Fin - ger, mein gol - de - nes Rin - ge -
ring up - on my fin - ger, My dear lit - tle ring of

lein, ich drü - cke dich fromm an die Lip - pen, dich
gold, I press thee de - vot - ed - ly to my lips, De -

rit.   *a tempo*

fromm an die Lip - pen, an das Her - ze mein.
vot - ed - ly now up - on my heart I hold.

Ped.   *

Ped.   *

ET EXULTAVIT SPIRITUS MEUS
(And My Spirit Hath Rejoiced)

from *Magnificant*

Johann Sebastian Bach
(1685-1750)

Et ex - ul - ta - vit   spi - ri - tus   me - us,
And__ my   spir - it   hath__ re - joic - ed,

et ex - ul - ta - vit   spi - ri - tus   me - us,
and__ my   spir - it   hath__ re - joic - ed,

60

ri me-o, in De-o sa-lu-ta—ri me o.
ed in God,— re - joic - ed in God,— my Sav - iour,

Et ex-ul - ta - vit spi-ri-tus me-us: in De -
and my spir - it hath— re - joic-ed, re - joic -

-o sa-lu-ta - ri, sa-lu - ta - ri,
-ed, hath re - joic - ed, re - joic-ed in— God, in— God,

-ri me - o, in De - o sa - lu' - ta - ri,
__my Sav - iour, hath__ re - joic-ed in__ God, my Sav-iour,

in De - o sa - lu - ta - ri me - o, in De-o sa - lu - ta -
hath__ re - joic-ed in God, __ my Sav - iour, in God, my Sav-iour, my

ri me - o.
Sav - iour.

IMMER LEISER WIRD MEIN SCHLUMMER
(Ever Gentler Grows My Slumber)

Hermann Lingg

Johannes Brahms
(1833-1897)

Trau - me hör' ich dich ru - fen drauss vor mei - ner Thür,
dreams I hear thee oft, At my door - way call - ing soft:

Nie - mand wacht und öff - net dir,
No one wakes to ope for thee,

ich er - wach' und wei - ne bit - ter - lich, wei -
I a - wake, and weep heart-brok-en - ly, weep

- ne bit - ter - lich.
- heart - brok - en - ly.

64

Ja, ich wer - de ster - ben müs - sen,
Death for me I know that this _____ is,

ei - ne And - re wirst du küs - sen,
Some - one else will have thy kiss - es

wenn ich bleich und kalt, ____ bleich ___ und
When I'm cold and dumb, ____ cold ___ and

kalt. ___ Eh' die Mai - en - lüf - te weh'n, eh' die
dumb. ___ Once, be - fore the A - pril rain, Ere the

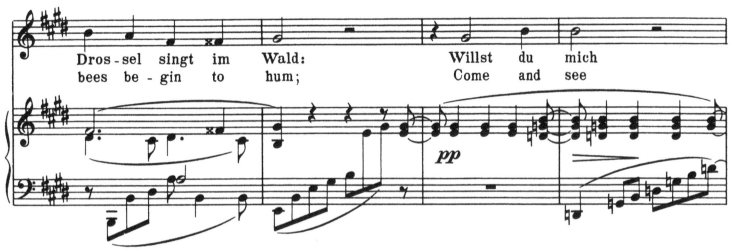

Dros-sel singt im Wald: Willst du mich
bees be-gin to hum; Come and see

noch ein-mal seh'n, komm', o
me once a-gain, Come, I

kom - - me bald, komm', o
beg ——— thee, come! Come, I

kom - - me bald!
beg thee, come!

L'HEURE EXQUISE
(The Exquisite Time)

Paul Verlaine
English version by Theodore Baker

Lady Dean Paul Poldowski
(Irena Regina Wieniawski)
(1880-1932)

68

ment   sem - ble   des - cen - - dre   Du   fir - ma -
lies   o'er   all   things   un - - der   yon   arch - ing

cresc.

ment   que   l'astre   i - ri - - se   c'est   l'heu - - re   ex -
skies   where   stars   are   gleam - - ing   this   hour - - of

p   morendo   dim.

qui - - se.
dream - - ing.

ppp   *legato*

rall.   **Lento**

de plus en plus loin

pp   *ppp*

LORD, LEAD ME IN THY RIGHTEOUSNESS

Luigi Cherubini
(1760-1842)

Lord, lead me in Thy right-eous-ness, de-fend me from mine en-e-mies; Make Thy way

O _____ hear ___ me, O

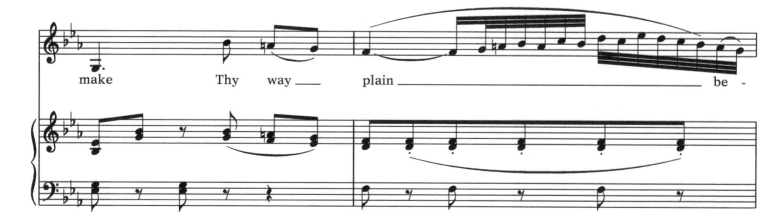

make Thy way ___ plain _____ be -

fore my _____ face.

Lord, lead me in Thy right-eous-ness, O hear me when I

call to Thee, and go not far a - way from me, make Thy way

plain _____ be - fore my face, and

go _____ not far, not ___ far _____ from

me, make Thy way plain _____ be - fore my face.

74

Lord, _____ lead me in Thy right - eous-ness,

O _____ hear me when I call _____ to Thee,

O _____ lead _____ me,

make   Thy   way

plain be - fore _____ my

face, and go _____ not

far a - way from_ me, O hear me when _____ I ___

call _____ to Thee

LORD TO THEE, EACH NIGHT AND DAY

from *Theodora*

George Frederic Handel
(1685-1759)

Lord, to Thee, each night and day, Strong in hope we

sing and pray strong in hope we sing and pray, each night and

79

Dal Segno al Fine

LUNGI DA TE

Giovanni Bononcini
(1670-1747)

Lungi da te ben mio
Morto al piacer son io,
Son vivo al mio dolor,

Far away from you, my love,
I am dead to pleasure,
Alive to every pain.

E pur la speme io sento
Dirmi: Sarai contento, se torni a riveder
Sull' ali del pensier

Yet the voice of hope is saying
Turn and look again –
In the magic cup of memory,

L'og - get - to del tuo a - mor,_____

l'og - get - to del tuo a - mor,_____

l'og - get - to del tuo a - mor._____

L'oggetto del tuo amor.

You will see your love.

DIE MAINACHT
(The May Night)

Ludwig Hölty
English version by Paul England

Johannes Brahms
(1833-1897)

flö - tet, wandl' ich trau - rig von Busch zu
war - bles, Sad I wan - der from tree to

Busch.
tree.

Ü - ber - hül - let vom
Some - where, hid in the

Laub gir - ret ein Tau - ben-paar sein Ent - zü - cken mir
leaves, soft - ly a pair of doves coo their love song to

vor; a - ber ich
me. Heart - sick I

wen - de mich,
turn a - way,
su - che dunk - le - re
Turn to shades that are

Schat - ten,
dark - er,
und
And
die
there

ein - sa - me Thrä - ne
wells but a sin - gle

rinnt.
tear.
Wann o lä - cheln-des
Where o vi - sion of

MON JARDIN
(My Garden)

André Alexandre
English version by Harry Goldby

Félix Fourdrain
(1880-1923)

Lento

Mon jar - din est plein de pen - sé - - es,
Here's my gar - den so full of pan - sies,

Co - rol - les clai - res ou fon - cées,
pe - tals dark red oth - ers bright blue,

Dou - ces à la main Com - me du sa - tin. De
Soft touch - ing the hand like sat - in or silk. Of

Cédez

si jo - lis tons nu - an - cé - es, Mon jar - din ___ est plein de pen -
so man - y shades and nu - an - ces, that's my gar - den, Oh, so full of

a tempo

sé - ces.
pan - sies.

Et ces fleurs, je ne sais com -
And these flowers oh how I do

ment, ___
mar - vel

El - les ont la for - me vrai - ment
that they take the shape that re - calls

Des
the

coif - fes d'Al - sa - ce, Ru - bans qu'a-vec grâ - ce
coifs of Al-sace, and their rib - bons so charm - ing.

Mes pa - y - ses, fil - les des
Now I see my house and my

allargando   a tempo

champs,   Por - tent sur leurs fronts   de vingt ans. _____
fields,   *And then all the girls   twen - ty years   young.*

f

rit.   a tempo
p

Co - rol - les clai - res   ou   fon - cé - es, O
Pet - als so light and   pet - als dark __ oh

p

coif - fes d'Al - sa - ce,   ô   pen - sées! _____
coifs of Al - sace _____   oh   my   pan -

8va

sies!

NEBBIE
(Mists)

Ada Negri
English version by Lorraine Noel Finley

Ottorino Respighi
(1879-1936)

94

QUI SEDES
(Who Sittest?)
from *Gloria*

Antonio Vivaldi
(1678-1741)

Allegro

Qui se - - - test des ad
Who sit - test at the

dex - - te - ram Pa - tris,
right _____ hand of the Fa - ther,

mi - se - re -
Lord, have mer -

cresc.

- re,
- cy,

f

mi - se - re - re, mi - se - re - re ____
Lord, have mer - cy, mer - cy, ___ Lord, up -

____ no - bis.
- *on us.*

f

Qui se - des ad
Who sit - test ad be -

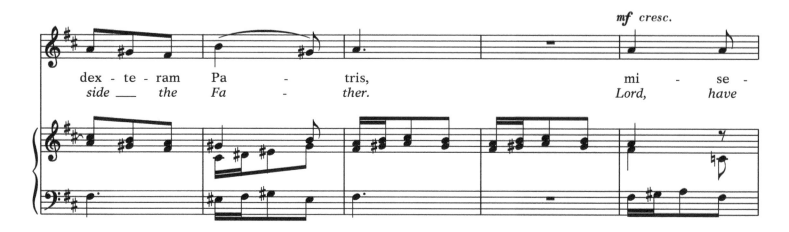

dex - te - ram Pa - tris, mi - se -
side ___ the Fa - ther. Lord, have

re - - - - - - - re no - bis,
mer - - - - - - - cy up - on ___ us,

-te - ram Pa - tris, mi - se - re -
hand of the Fa - ther, Lord, have mer

re,
cy,

mi - se - re - re, mi - se -
Lord, ____ have mer - cy, mer - cy,

re - re _____ no - bis,
Lord, up - on us,

mi - se - re - re, mi - se - re - re, mi - se -
Lord, have mer - cy, Lord, have mer - cy, mer - cy,

re - re no - bis.
Lord, up - on us.

senza rit.

SE TU DELLA MIA MORTE
(Would'st Thou the Boast of Ending)

Alessandro Scarlatti
(1660-1725)

English version by Dr. Theodore Baker

Se tu_____ del-la mia mor - te a que-sta de-stra
Would'st thou_____ the boast of end - ing A life and love of -

for - te la glo-ria non vuoi dar, dal - la a' tuoi lu _ _ mi, dal _ _
fend - ing De-ny to this right hand; Grant it to thine own eyes, grant

SERENITY

John Greenleaf Whittier

Charles Ives
(1874-1954)

Very slowly, quietly and sustained, with little
or no change in tempo or volume throughout.

SONG OF DEVOTION

Adapted from
Philippians 1:3-11

John Ness Beck
(1930-1987)

And this I pray, that your love may a - bound yet more and more. in

knowl-edge and in all judg-ment, that ye may ap - prove things that are ex - cel-lent, that

poco a poco cresc.

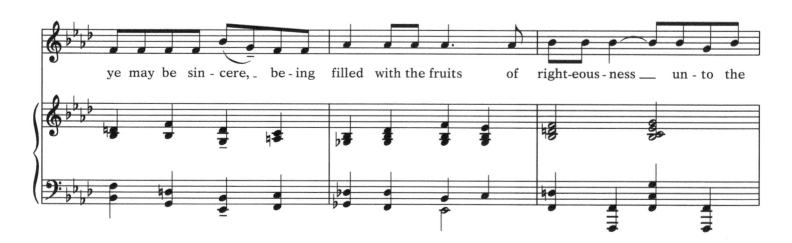

ye may be sin - cere, be-ing filled with the fruits of right-eous-ness un - to the

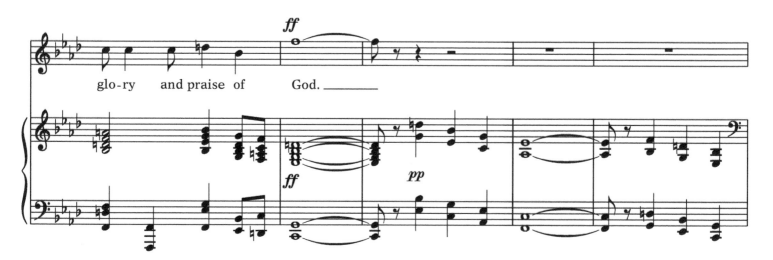

glo-ry and praise of God.

I thank my God _____ on ev-'ry re-

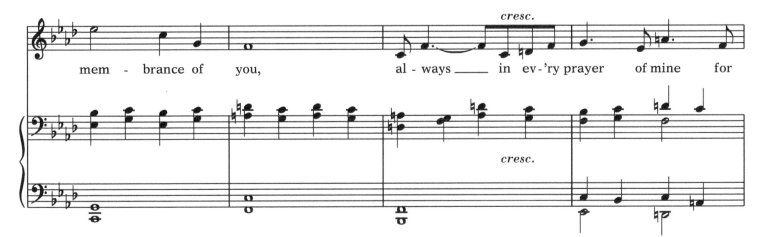

mem - brance of you, al - ways ____ in ev-'ry prayer of mine for

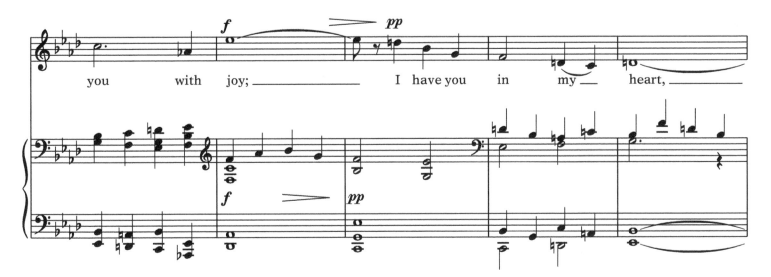

you with joy; _____ I have you in my ___ heart, _____

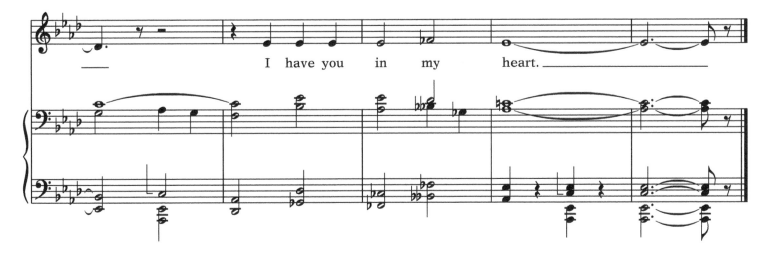

____ I have you in my heart. _____

SONG OF THE OPEN

Jessica Hawley Lowell

Frank La Forge
(1879-1953)

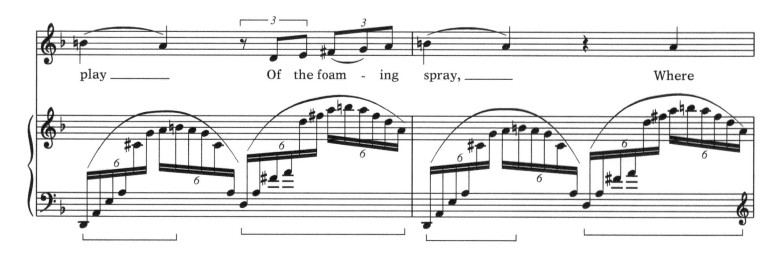

play _____ Of the foam - ing spray, _____ Where

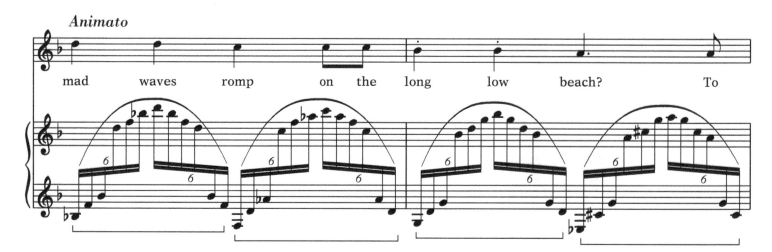

Animato

mad waves romp on the long low beach? To

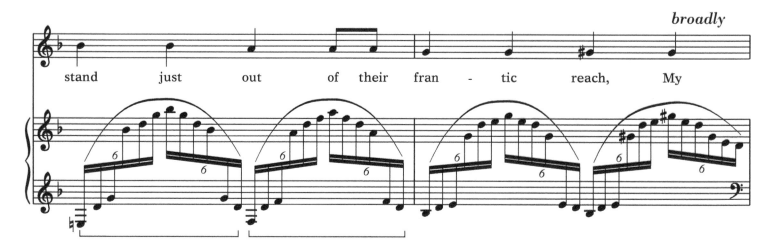

broadly

stand just out of their fran - tic reach, My

hair blown free and the breath of me Caught

a tempo   *, broadly*

hard   in   the   pas - sion - ate   breath   of   the   sea,   With   your

hands _____ in   mine   it   were

senza rit.   *Vivo*

ec -   sta - sy!

LA SPERANZA È GIUNTA
(Spring)
from *Otho*

English version by Arthur Somervell

George Frideric Handel
(1685-1759)

Andante con moto

La spe-ran - za è giun - ta in por - to
Spring is com-ing With sun and _ shower and blos-som.

non legato

*Optional abbreviated introduction, cut to **.

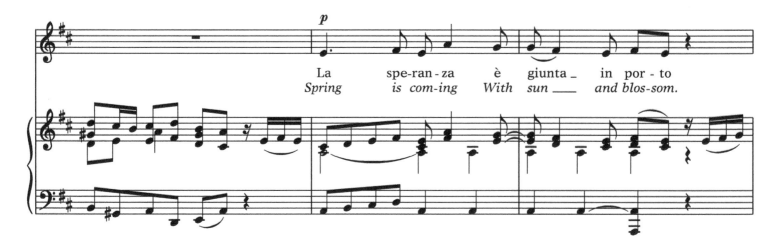

La spe-ran-za è giunta in por-to
Spring is com-ing With sun and blos-som.

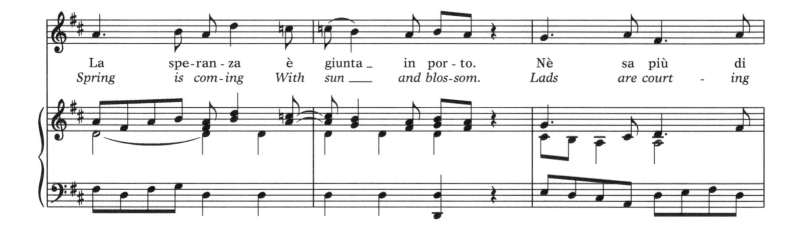

La spe-ran-za è giunta in por-to. Nè sa più di
Spring is com-ing With sun and blos-som. Lads are court - ing

che te-me-re Se tran-quil-lo ve-de il mar
Lambs are sport - ing, Birds are sing - ing, I hear them sing - ing

ve - de il mar Se tran-quil - lo ve - de il mar.
Their car-ols ring - ing, Their car-ols ring - ing on ev - 'ry tree.

Nè   sa più   di
Birds   are sing-ing   I

che   te - me - re   Se   tran-quil - lo ve - de il mar.
hear   their car - ols ring-ing from ev - 'ry tree.

TEARS

Wang Seng-Ju
(6th Century)

Charles T. Griffes
(1884-1920)

High o'er the hill ___ the moon-barque steers. ___

The lan - - tern lights de-part. ___

Dead springs are stir - - ring in ___ my heart;

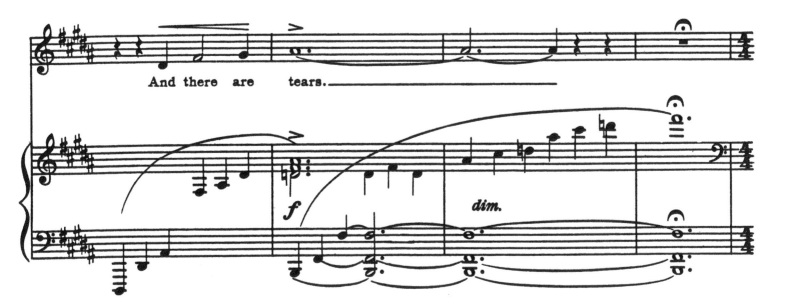

And there are tears._____

Poco più mosso   *cresc.*

But that which makes my grief more deep,_____ Is that

Tempo Iº   *dim.*   *rit.*

you   know____ not when I weep._____

THE TWENTY-THIRD PSALM

Albert Hay Malotte
(1865-1924)

Quietly and peacefully ♩ = 72

He mak-eth me to lie down in green pas - tures:

he lead-eth me beside the still wa - ters. He re-

stor - eth my soul: he lead-eth me in the paths of right-eous-ness for

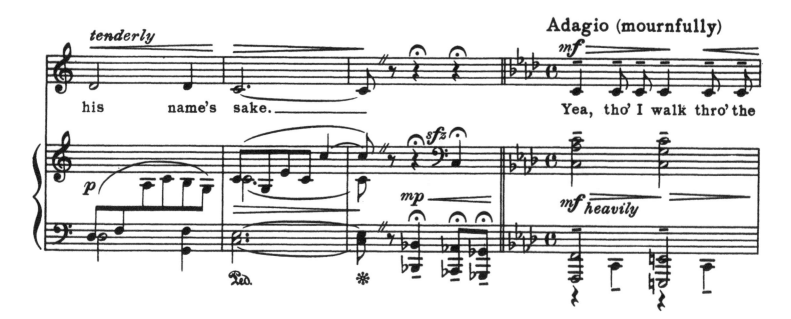

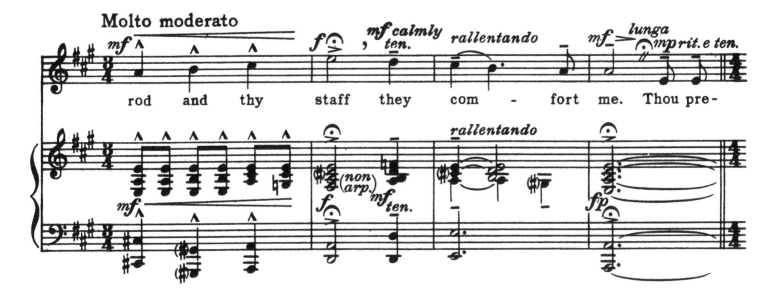

rod and thy staff they com - fort me. Thou pre-

par-est a ta-ble be-fore me in the pres-ence of mine en - e - mies:

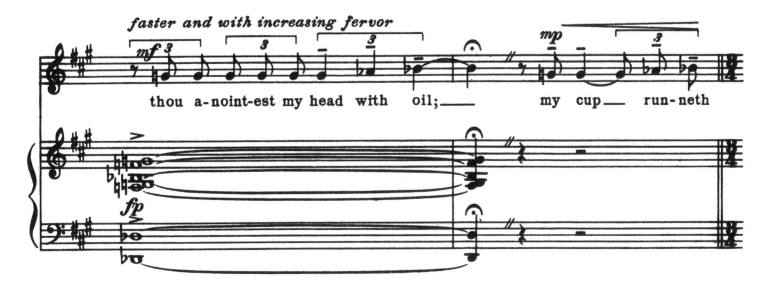

thou a-noint-est my head with oil;___ my cup___ run-neth

124

Very slowly and with great feeling

ral-len-tan - do

in the house of the Lord for

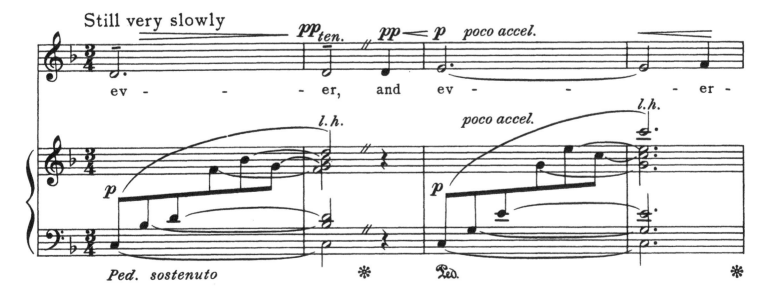

Still very slowly

ev - - - er, and ev - - - - er -

Ped. sostenuto

Tempo I° ♩= 72

more.

pp gradually slower and dying__ away____

WHEN A MERRY MAIDEN MARRIES

from *The Gondoliers*

W.S. Gilbert

Arthur Sullivan
(1842-1900)

af - ter   Let our tears be tears of laugh - ter.   Ev - 'ry sigh that finds a

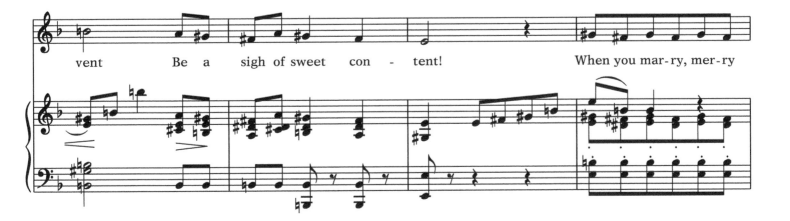

vent   Be a   sigh of sweet con - tent!   When you mar-ry, mer-ry

rall.   *a tempo sostenuto*

maid - en,   Then the air with love is lad - en; Ev - 'ry flow'r is a

p

rose, Ev - 'ry goose be - comes a swan,   Ev - 'ry kind of trou - ble

128

goes Where the last year's snows have gone! Sun-light takes the place of

shade ___ When you mar-ry, mer-ry maid. ___ When a mer-ry maid-en

mar - ries, Sor - row goes and pleas-ure tar - ries; Ev - 'ry sound be-comes a

song, All is right and noth - ing's wrong!

When a mer-ry maid-en mar - ries

Sor-row goes and pleas-ure tar - ries; Ev -'ry sound be-comes a song All is

right and noth-ing's wrong. Gnaw-ing Care and ach-ing Sor - row

Get ye gone un - til to - mor - row; Jeal-ous-ies in grim ar - ray, Ye are

things of yes - ter - day! When you mar-ry mer-ry maid - en,

rall.　　　　　　　　　*a tempo, sostenuto*

Then the air with joy is lad - en; All the cor-ners of the earth Ring with

mu - sic sweet-ly played, Wor-ry is mel - o - dious mirth, Grief is

p

joy in mas-que-rade; Sul-len night is laugh-ing day ___

All the year is mer-ry May Ah   All the year is mer-ry May, ___

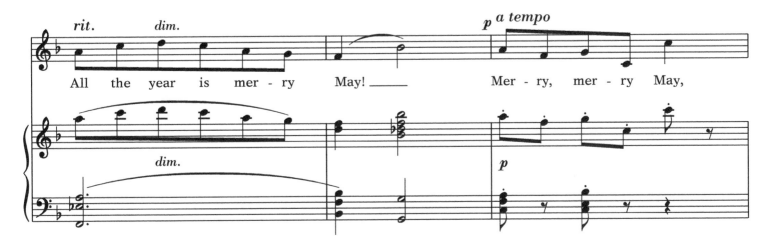

All the year is mer-ry May! ___   Mer-ry, mer-ry May,

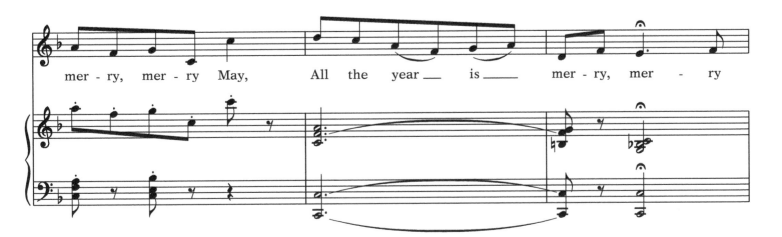

mer-ry, mer-ry May,   All the year ___ is ___   mer-ry, mer-ry

May.

WHEN FREDERIC WAS A LITTLE LAD

from *The Pirates of Penzance*

W.S. Gilbert

Arthur Sullivan
(1842-1900)

har - dy lad, though _ sure - ly not a high lot, Though
was to make, and _ doom him to a vile lot, I
find me now, a _ mem - ber of your shy lot, Which you

I'm a nurse, you might do worse than make your boy a a
bound him to a pi - rate _ you! — in - stead of to a a
would-n't have found, had he been bound ap - pren - tice to a a

1, 2
pi - lot!
pi - lot!

3
pi - lot!

WHERE THE MUSIC COMES FROM

Lee Hoiby
(b. 1926)

wake to the liv-ing spir - it Here in - side me where it lies. I want to

lis - ten till I can hear it, Let it guide me, and re - al - ize That I can

go with the flow un - end - ing, That is blend - ing, that is

real; And oh, _____ I want to

feel.

I want to

walk in the earth-ly gar - den, Far from cit-ies, far from

fear. I want to talk to the grow-ing gar - den, To the

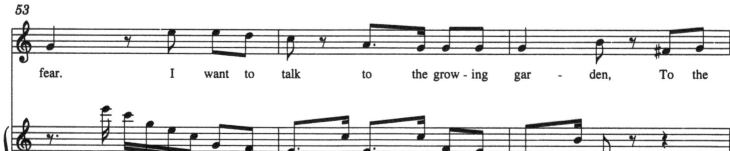

* pronounced *day – vas* (nature spirits)